FIGHTING
TO SURVIVE
ANIMAL ATTACKS
TERRIFYING TRUE STORIES

By Nancy Dickmann

COMPASS POINT BOOKS
a capstone imprint

Compass Point Books are published by Capstone Press
1710 Roe Crest Drive, North Mankato, Minnesota 56003
www.capstonepub.com

Library of Congress Cataloging-in-Publication Data
Names: Dickmann, Nancy, author.
Title: Fighting to survive animal attacks : terrifying true stories / by Nancy Dickmann.
Description: North Mankato, Minnesota : Compass Point Books, [2020] | Series:
   Fighting to survive | Audience: Age 10–14. | Audience: Grade 4–8. |
   Includes bibliographical references and index.
Identifiers: LCCN 2019007684| ISBN 9780756561840 (library binding) | ISBN
   9780756562311 (paperback) | ISBN 9780756562069 (ebook pdf)
Subjects: LCSH: Animal attacks—Juvenile literature.
Classification: LCC QL100.5 .D53 2020 | DDC 591.5/3—dc23
LC record available at https://lccn.loc.gov/2019007684

Editorial Credits
Gena Chester, editor; Terri Poburka, designer; Morgan Walters, media researcher;
Kathy McColley, production specialist

Photo Credits
Alamy: David South, 51; Getty Images: Bates Littlehales, 23, Fairfax Media, 28, STF, 45,
TIM SLOAN, 37; iStockphoto: seread, (bear) Cover; Newscom: Orange County Register/
ZUMAPRESS, 58; Shutterstock: Alexius Sutandio, 27, Amanda Wayne, 20, Bardocz Peter,
31, Brian A. Witkin, 9, GUDKOV ANDREY, 33, 34, Gustavo Miguel Fernandes, 12, Isaac
Marzioli, (ink) design element throughout, Jim Agronick, 25, kojihirano, 55, Martin
Mecnarowski, 41, Martin Voeller, 11, mikeledray, 48, Miloje, (paper) design element,
Peter Hermes Furian, 7, photomystery, 49, Rainer Lesniewski, 15, 39, 46, 53, Lesniewski,
39, Ric Campos, 4, Roger de la Harpe, 43, stockaboo, 18, Tom Reichner, 17, Warren
Metcalf, 57, xpixel, (grunge) design element throughout

TABLE OF
CONTENTS

INTRODUCTION

For people living in big cities, who rarely see anything more frightening than a squirrel or a pigeon, it's easy to forget how fierce nature can be. Each year thousands of people around the world are killed by animals. Millions more are injured—but they survive.

People often go out into the wilderness for fun activities, such as hiking, camping, mountain biking, or surfing. In addition, a growing world population means our cities and towns are spreading into areas that used to be wild. This puts humans and animals closer together. And the natural world can be a wild and dangerous place!

DEADLY ANIMALS

Only a few animal species, including lions, tigers, and sharks, hunt humans for food. Other large animals, such as hippos and elephants, also attack and kill people, but not to eat them. Smaller animals can dangerous too! Snakes, scorpions, bees, and even ants are all responsible for deaths. Animals don't even have to be wild to be dangerous—pet cats and dogs bite millions of people each year.

Some animals kill people indirectly by spreading disease. When they bite people, tsetse flies can pass on a disease known as "sleeping sickness." It kills thousands of people each year. A mosquito bite may be itchy and annoying, but it can also be deadly. A bite from an infected mosquito can pass on malaria or dengue fever, which kill hundreds of thousands of people each year.

WHY ATTACK?

Many animal attacks are a case of self-defense and happen when animals are surprised. They may be protecting their territory or their babies. Animals have different ways of protecting themselves. Jellyfish and scorpions can sting, while snakes bite and horses kick. Attacks also happen when food is scarce. When an animal is hungry and desperate, it is more likely to take risks—including attacking humans.

DEATH AND SURVIVAL

Although animal attacks are often reported on the news, the risk of being killed by an animal is very, very low compared to the chances of dying from disease or in a car accident. Most people survive animal attacks. Read on to discover some of the most thrilling stories of people who escaped with their lives!

BACK ON THE BOARD
BETHANY HAMILTON

For 13-year-old Bethany Hamilton, it was supposed to be just another fun morning out on the ocean. On October 31, 2003, she went surfing with her best friend, Alana. Alana's father and younger brother were with them. They were looking forward to catching some waves. But no one realized that morning would change Bethany's life forever.

BORN TO SURF

Bethany lived on the Hawaiian island of Kauai, where she had been born into a surfing family. Her mother, father, and two older brothers all surfed. Bethany would later remember learning to surf before she could walk.

Bethany started surfing competitively when she was only 8 years old—and she was good. By the time she was 9, she had her first sponsorship deal. In fact earlier that year, Bethany had traveled with her team to a competition in California. She finished second in the open women's division of the NSSA National Championships. She was strong and confident with no fear of the water.

SHATTERED CALM

That fateful morning Bethany and her friends had gone to Tunnels Beach and paddled out into the ocean to surf. At one point Bethany was lying on her stomach on her surfboard, waiting for a good wave. Her right arm was on the board and her left arm was trailing in the water. It was a peaceful early morning with sea turtles in the water.

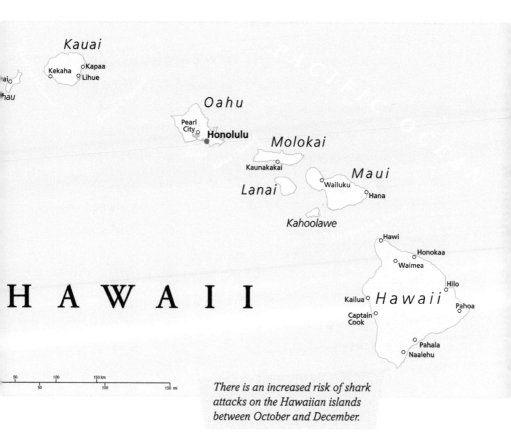

Kauai

Kekaha   Kapaa
       Lihue

O a h u

Pearl
City   **Honolulu**

M o l o k a i

Kaunakakai

Lanai   Wailuku   M a u i

      Hana

Kahoolawe

Hawi

Honokaa
Waimea

H A W A I I   Kailua   *H a w a i i*   Hilo

Captain   Pahoa
Cook

        Pahala
       Naalehu

There is an increased risk of shark attacks on the Hawaiian islands between October and December.

But then something grabbed her arm. Bethany felt intense pressure, and for a few seconds she was pulled back and forth. She grabbed onto her surfboard with her right hand, trying to avoid being pulled underwater. Then the pulling suddenly stopped—what had happened?

BLOOD IN THE WATER

Bethany didn't feel any pain, but she saw the water around her turn red. There was a large, semi-circular chunk missing from her surfboard. With a shock she realized that her left arm was gone. The red color staining the water was her own blood.

"I just got attacked by a shark!" she called out to her friends. At first, Alana's father, Holt, thought she was kidding. The attack had happened so quickly, and Bethany hadn't screamed or splashed. But as she tried to paddle toward the others with just one arm, they saw the blood in the water. Their sunny morning on the waves had turned into a nightmare.

RACE TO SHORE

Blood was pumping out of the wound where the shark had bitten Bethany. They were still a few hundred yards from shore. If she had any chance of survival, they needed to stop the bleeding quickly. And they needed to get out of the water—the shark could still be nearby.

Holt wrapped his t-shirt tightly around what was left of her arm. There was no sign of the missing limb in the water. Bethany did her best to stay calm. She reminded herself that if she panicked, she could put herself in more danger. Holt led the group back to shore, pulling Bethany along on her surfboard.

Once they were back on dry land, Holt used a rubber surfboard leash as a tourniquet, trying to stop the flow of blood. They called an ambulance and waited anxiously for it to arrive. It would take about an hour to get to the hospital—would Bethany survive that long?

HOSPITAL COINCIDENCE

Bethany's father, Tom, happened to be at the local hospital that morning. He had no idea what had happened to Bethany. Instead he was being prepped for a routine operation on his knee. But before they could start, a doctor came in to tell him that he'd been bumped down the priority list. A badly injured surfer was on the way in an ambulance, and she would take his spot on the operating table.

Tom Hamilton knew his daughter had been out on the water that morning. "Oh please . . . not my daughter?" he asked the surgeon. The doctor admitted Bethany had been the victim of a serious shark attack.

Bethany Hamilton competing at the Super Girl Pro in California.

AT THE HOSPITAL

When Bethany's ambulance arrived, she was raced into the operating room, and doctors began working on her immediately. She had lost about 60 percent of her blood, and needed transfusions to save her life. Bethany would later remember she felt no pain in the ambulance—just numbness.

The surgeons discovered that only about four inches of the bone in Bethany's upper arm remained. After getting her into a stable condition, they performed more operations to repair the damage caused by the shark. Once they finished, Bethany was left with a very small stump where her arm had once been.

CATCHING THE SHARK

When the story of Bethany's attack made the news, people were horrified. They wanted the shark that was responsible to be caught. Tom Hamilton spoke to a friend, a fisherman and fellow surfer, and asked him to try to catch the shark. He was worried that if it wasn't caught, it might attack other surfers. Tom's friend and another man finally succeeded in catching a 14-foot (4.3-meter) tiger shark, not far from where Bethany had been attacked. When they compared its jaws to the bite mark on her surfboard, they matched.

a tiger shark

DID YOU KNOW?

The shark that bit Bethany was a tiger shark. These large, aggressive sharks can grow up to 18 feet (5.5 m) in length. They are top predators that feed on squid, seals, sea turtles, dolphins, and even other sharks. Tiger sharks often visit shallow reefs and harbors. They are responsible for more shark attacks on humans than any species, other than great white sharks.

Bethany Hamilton competing in the Rip Curl Pro in Portugal in 2010.

RECOVERY

After several days in the hospital, Bethany was released and allowed to go home. Everything would be more difficult now, as she slowly got used to life with just one arm. But there was one thing she was certain about—she wanted to surf again.

Within a month Bethany was back on her surfboard. It was difficult at first. With one arm missing, her center of balance was different, and that took some getting used to. It was also harder to "pop up"—a move used by surfers to go from lying down to standing up on the board. With only one arm to push up with, Bethany needed to change her technique. She had a new board custom-made with a handle for her right arm.

SUCCESS!

Just months after the attack, Bethany entered a surfing competition. Many people were surprised to see her competing again so soon, but her friends and family weren't fazed. Bethany had always been incredibly strong and determined, and surfing was her life.

In the years that followed, she won or placed in several major competitions. She wrote a book about her experience, which was turned into a Hollywood movie titled *Soul Surfer.* There was nothing that would have stopped her from achieving her dream of becoming a successful, professional surfer—not even a shark attack.

INTO THE WOODS
PETER BACA

Peter Baca was looking forward to his first-ever camping trip. He lived in Tempe, near Phoenix, Arizona, and considered himself a city boy. But with Father's Day and his son's first birthday falling near the same time, it seemed like a perfect opportunity for the family to give camping a try.

For their trip Baca and his girlfriend chose the Tonto National Forest in central Arizona. This 3-million-acre wilderness is full of stunning natural beauty. The Ponderosa Campground, where Baca set up their tent, is surrounded by trees. It lies on the Mogollon Rim, a 200-mile- (322-kilometer-) long cliff cutting across the state. It was late June, and the weather was beautiful. The skies were clear and blue, and the crisp scent of pine filled the air.

DANGEROUS GROUND

Baca didn't know bears in the forest had edged closer and closer to the campgrounds. Black bears are generally shy, but they have a reputation for raiding campsites in search of food, especially during times of drought. Arizona had been very dry that year, and there had been several wildfires as well. These natural occurrences affected the feeding grounds of the bears that lived in the forest. In search of food, they moved out of their normal areas and closer to the campgrounds.

When they set up camp, Baca and his girlfriend had no idea that just three weeks earlier, a black bear had attacked a woman in that very campground. It had ripped open her tent and clawed her leg—but she survived. There had been a second attack just the night before about 1.5 miles (2.4 km) away. A bear broke into a cabin and bit a sleeping man on the leg. The same bear might have been behind both attacks, but no bears had been caught.

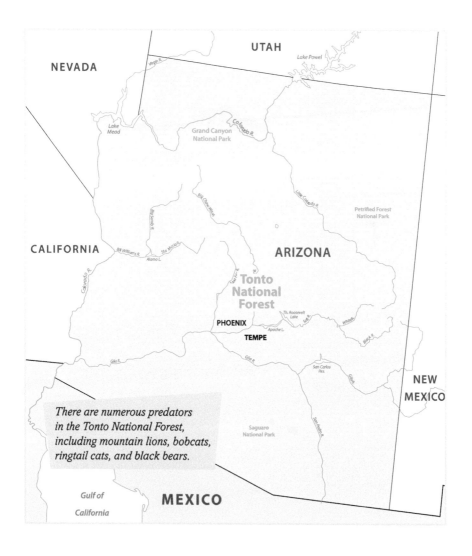

There are numerous predators in the Tonto National Forest, including mountain lions, bobcats, ringtail cats, and black bears.

ATTACK AT DAWN

After a peaceful night's sleep, the calm was shattered around dawn. Baca awoke with a start, feeling pain in his arm. The early morning sunlight filtering through the tent revealed a large, dark figure. Then he looked down in shock at his arm—the flesh was bloody and mangled. There was a bear's head poking through the window of the tent!

TRAIL OF DESTRUCTION

Baca's tent was not the first one the bear had visited. A few minutes earlier at the other end of the campground, the bear ripped a hole in Kim Bress's tent. She saw the bear looking at her, and she grabbed her children. Her husband shouted at the bear, scaring it away. The bear visited and shook the next tent as well. Hearing the noise, Carly and Steve Stoltenberg raced out of their tent close by to try and scare the bear away. They yelled and waved their arms, and the bear lumbered off—but it headed straight for Baca's tent.

TUG OF WAR

The bear tore and tugged at Baca's arm. Dizzy with pain, he shouted out to his girlfriend, telling her to grab the baby and run. While Baca fought against the bear, she was able to gather up baby Gabriel and get out of the tent. In fear for her partner's life, she raced off to find help.

a black bear

DID YOU KNOW?

Black bears are the only species of wild bear found in Arizona.
These bears are smaller than their cousins, the grizzly bears.
Even so, a large male can stand 6 feet (183 centimeters) tall
and weigh up to 600 pounds (272 kilograms).

SLOW MOTION

Baca engaged in a life-or-death struggle with the bear. He later recalled that things seemed to move in slow motion. As he tried to free himself from the bear's jaws, the bear used its powerful jaws, as well as its razor-sharp claws, to attack Baca. It moved up his arm, tearing out a large chunk of flesh.

Baca was doing his best to fight the bear off with his uninjured arm, but the bear was large and powerful. And Baca was losing a lot of blood, leaving him weak and in shock.

Usually bears attack humans to protect their young or food source or if they're startled. Bears rarely attack because they think humans are their food source.

MANGLED FLESH

Only minutes had passed, but to Baca it felt like hours of desperate struggle. Then the bear stood up, dragging Baca with it. It let go of his arm, but then began biting his head. Baca screamed for help as the bear bit and tore at his scalp.

Bears have powerful jaws, capable of snapping bones with a single bite. Baca was lucky—the bear seemed to bite only his scalp, and not his skull. But the bear was still causing tremendous damage. It nearly ripped off one of Baca's ears entirely. Blood was pouring down Baca's face, running into his swollen eyes, leaving it difficult to see.

RESCUE AT LAST

It was harder and harder for Baca to fight back. He was weak from lack of blood and the shock caused by his horrific injuries. Then, through a haze of pain, he heard shots fired. It was a small-caliber weapon, not powerful enough to bring down a bear. But thankfully the noise of the shots distracted the bear.

MEDICAL EMERGENCY

Other campers were shouting and throwing things, trying to scare the bear away. Eventually it let go of Baca and ran off into the forest, where it disappeared into the trees. But Baca's ordeal was far from over. The tent collapsed around him, and he struggled to find a way out. He was bleeding heavily and could barely stand. He could see the horrified expressions on the faces of the other campers. He knew he must be in very bad shape.

A black bear can smell food at campsites at least 1 mile (1.6 km) away.

Baca tried to get to his truck, but he had no strength left. Luckily one of the other people visiting the campsite was an off-duty Emergency Medical Technician (EMT). He had an advanced first aid kit with him. The EMT immediately realized Baca was in danger of bleeding to death. He wrapped up Baca's head wounds in an attempt to stop the bleeding. Then he set up an IV to replace some of the fluids Baca had lost.

RECOVERY

It took about 30 minutes for a helicopter to arrive and take Baca to a hospital. Without the quick actions of the off-duty EMT, he might not have lasted that long. When Baca woke up at the hospital, he instinctively tried to fight the bear before realizing that he was safe. But what about his family? His thoughts immediately turned to his 1-year-old son. Thankfully Gabriel had escaped without a scratch.

Doctors stitched up his injuries and did their best with the gaping hole in Baca's arm. He eventually recovered from the attack, though he will carry the scars from the attack for the rest of his life. They are not his only permanent marks. Baca had a bear tattooed on his shoulder as a reminder of his epic battle for survival.

BELLY OF THE BEAST
ERIC NERHUS

The great white shark is one of nature's top predators. These fearsome fish that terrified movie-goers in the *Jaws* films have a reputation for deadly attacks. Although they prefer to eat seals and dolphins, they do sometimes attack humans. Not many people escape to tell the tale, but Eric Nerhus is one of the lucky ones.

DIVING DEEP

The day of the attack started just like any other. Eric Nerhus, a 41-year-old professional diver, swam through the waters off Cape Howe about 12.5 miles (20 km) south of his hometown of Eden, Australia. Nerhus was diving for a shellfish called abalone, while his 25-year-old son, Mark, piloted the support boat. It was a warm, clear day, but the seas were a bit rough. Many of his fellow divers had decided not to go in the water that morning.

RISKY BUSINESS

Abalone diving is a dangerous job, but it's one that can provide huge rewards. These large shellfish are a type of sea snail that attach themselves to rocks in shallow waters. Divers harvest abalone by prying them off the rocks with metal tools. Abalone meat is considered a delicacy in Asia. Their beautiful shells are used to make jewelry and other items.

Buyers will pay top prices for abalones, but harvesting them is not always safe. Divers often spend 6–8 hours underwater searching for the shellfish. During that time, they share the waters with dangerous creatures—including great white sharks. Encounters are common, and some of them have been fatal.

The most dangerous times for divers are when they are descending from, or returning to, their boat. This is because great white sharks usually attack their prey from below. They swim up quickly and slam into their prey with their jaws open.

a diver harvesting abalone off the coast of California

THE BEAST APPROACHES

Nerhus was swimming just above the sea floor at a depth of about 25 feet (7.6 m). He was in an area he had dived many times before. Strict regulations meant he could only take abalone above a certain size. Nerhus swam along with his head down, following a line of abalone on the sea floor. Rough waters were kicking up sand and silt, making visibility poor. He was concentrating on deciding whether or not the shellfish he could see were big enough to harvest.

Nerhus never saw the shark approaching. Then something slammed into him—hard! Nerhus didn't realize at first what had happened to him. It was like he was in a dark cave with something squashing him like a vise.

IN THE JAWS OF A MONSTER

The pressure and darkness were intense. Then reality dawned on him—he was inside a shark! The enormous great white shark had swallowed him headfirst. Now his head, shoulders, and one arm were inside the shark's throat. Its sharp teeth were crunching into his torso. Nerhus realized that only his hips and legs remained outside the animal's body. He was facing every abalone diver's worst nightmare—being eaten alive by a great white!

a great white shark

DID YOU KNOW?

Great white sharks can grow up to 20 feet (6 m) or more in length. Only the basking shark and whale shark are bigger.

FIGHT FOR SURVIVAL

Nerhus had been breathing oxygen through a regulator in his mouth, but the attack knocked it out. Without oxygen, his situation became even more desperate. He could only survive for a minute or so without it. One arm was trapped inside the shark and one outside. In the darkness he couldn't find the regulator.

Nerhus had even bigger problems. The shark had a firm grip on his body, and it was starting to shake him. He knew enough about sharks to realize that this was serious. When a great white shark shakes its prey, it is trying to cut off the biggest piece of meat it can get. The shark was trying to use the force of its jaws, combined with a powerful shaking motion, to cut Nerhus in half.

SAVED BY THE VEST?

The wetsuit that Nerhus was wearing was no match for the shark's jaws. Luckily he was also wearing a lead-weighted vest. This piece of scuba equipment allows divers to stay deep below the surface for long periods. The razor-sharp teeth of the great white had a hard time penetrating the lead-lined vest.

Even with the vest's protection, Nerhus was in serious trouble. Some of the shark's teeth were still digging deep into his flesh. And he still had no oxygen supply. Years of working as a professional diver meant he was strong and tough. He would need every ounce of strength and ingenuity to escape the shark.

FIGHTING BACK

Never in his life had Nerhus felt fear like he experienced now. But he knew if he wanted to survive, he had to fight back. With his left hand, which was outside the shark, he felt along the side of the shark's head. His fingers moved along until he reached the shark's eye socket. Then, with his abalone chisel, he began to jab as hard as he could at the shark's eye.

Sharks have sensitive eyes, snouts, and gills. If you're ever under attack, those are the first places you should hit.

ESCAPE FROM THE JAWS

The attack on the shark's eye made its mouth open a little bit. Nerhus grabbed the opportunity and tried to wiggle out. But the shark wouldn't give up easily. As the diver tried to frantically to pull his head out of the creature's mouth, its bite crushed his dive mask onto his face. The force of the impact broke Nerhus' nose.

Then, at last, he was out! The first thing Nerhus did was to grab his regulator and put it back in. Now he could breathe again. But the ordeal wasn't over—the shark was still right there, excited by the pool of blood that was in the water.

Emergency responders rush Nerhus to the hospital.

RESCUE

Nerhus tried to stay as calm as possible. He swam for the surface, trying not to kick or splash too much. The shark swam around and around his feet in tight circles, staring at him without any hint of fear.

Nerhus broke the surface and shouted for help. He feared he would feel the shark's jaws on his legs at any moment. Luckily Mark was not far away in the support boat. Mark pulled his father out of the water. Nerhus was bleeding—but alive. Two divers from another boat gave Nerhus first aid and called for emergency help.

STITCHES AND SCARS

A helicopter took Nerhus to the hospital, where doctors treated his wounds. He had lost a lot of blood, and at least 14 of the shark's teeth had penetrated his lead vest. But since the vest kept the sharks teeth from going in too far, none of the wounds were deeper than about an inch. There were scratches and punctures along his shoulders and chest. In total Nerhus needed 75 stitches. Amazingly only a few months later, he was back in the water diving for abalone!

TUSKS OF TERROR
MICHAEL FAY

The wilderness held no fear for Michael Fay. In his career as a researcher and conservationist, he spent years exploring nature. Fay had faced tropical diseases, armed poachers, and even a plane crash. He'd survived them all. But one of his narrowest escapes came from one of the animals he worked to protect—the African forest elephant.

THE MEGATRANSECT

Fay felt at home in the rain forests of central Africa. In 1999 he embarked on a challenging expedition that he called the "Megatransect." With a small team, he set off to walk through the Congo River Basin. His path would cover 2,000 miles (3,219 km) from the Republic of the Congo to the Gabon coast. It took his team 456 days to walk the entire distance through thick tropical rain forests.

Throughout the long journey, Fay's team photographed and studied the plants and animals they encountered. Trekking through the jungle gave Fay valuable experience with how to deal with wild animals. They encountered gorillas and crocodiles, as well as smaller pests such as biting insects.

HELPING WILDLIFE

Fay and his team saw how human activity affected the landscape and its wildlife. This research helped him figure out which areas of wilderness were in most need of protection. At the end of the journey, the data they collected was put to good use. Fay helped convince the president of Gabon, El Hadj Omar Bongo, to create a national park system. Thirteen areas in the country were set aside to protect wildlife. Together they covered more than 11,000 square miles (28,500 square km). But Fay nearly didn't see this dream realized.

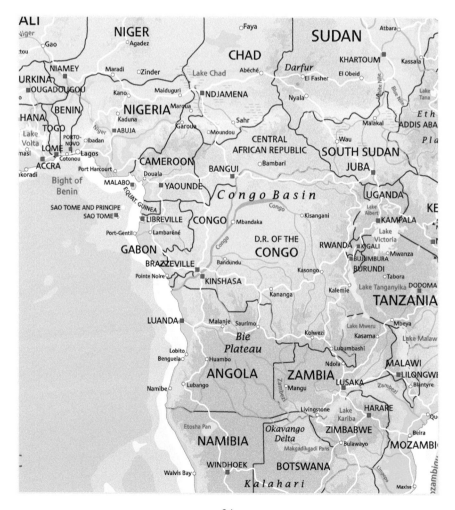

A VICIOUS ATTACK

It was New Year's Eve in 2002. Gabon's national park system would be legally created in about a week's time. Fay was with a group of friends at one of the newly-created parks. In fact he was at the very place he had finished his Megatransect about two years earlier. It was a time to celebrate friendship and new beginnings.

However, Fay and his friends soon encountered a group of African forest elephants in the area, and the elephants were not happy. African forest elephants are normally peaceful animals, but something had spooked or angered them. They began to move around and encircled Fay and his friends. This was a typical elephant maneuver Fay recognized right away.

One elephant, a large female, held back while the others in her group approached. Fay spotted her but assumed she was out of the picture. But then she came flying out of the woods, heading straight for him.

DEFENDING THE DEFENDER

For years, Fay had been a defender of elephants. He'd seen firsthand the effects of poachers who killed elephants for their ivory tusks. He made it one of his goals to protect these beautiful, intelligent animals. But now he would have to protect himself from them.

African forest elephants

DID YOU KNOW?

There are about 100,000 forest elephants in the world, and most of them live in Gabon. For a long time, these giants were considered to be the same species as the more familiar African bush elephant. But the tusks of African forest elephants are straighter and point downward. They use their hard, sharp tusks to push their way through dense forests.

SIZE AND STRENGTH

African forest elephants are the smallest species of elephant, but they are significantly bigger and heavier than a human. The one running at Fay was about 7 feet (213 cm) tall at the shoulder and weighed several tons. She had 16-inch (41-cm) tusks that ended in deadly sharp points.

Fay knew the best way to deal with an elephant attack was to stand your ground and make noise. Usually this will make a person look dangerous and frighten the elephant away. Fay tried this tactic, but the elephant kept coming. He got the rest of his group, including his girlfriend, behind him.

FRONTAL ATTACK

The elephant had her head down and her ears tucked back—a sure sign of aggression. She was about to charge.

Fay knew exactly how dangerous an angry elephant could be. In the few seconds available to him, he weighed his options. Should he try to stand his ground and fight? Or should he try to run?

An elephant is fast, but it can't change direction quickly. With a head start, running in a zig-zag pattern can sometimes work to evade a charging elephant. Fay decided to run, but after just a few steps he tripped. He went flying and landed on his stomach on the ground.

PLUNGING TUSKS

Fay immediately rolled over onto his back. The elephant was nearly on top of him. Her deadly tusks pointed at his chest just a foot away. Fay made a frantic grab for the tusks and guided them past his body. One of them slammed into the sand—inches from his head. Fay found himself eye-to-eye with a giant elephant intent on killing him.

African forest elephants normally avoid humans, but shrinking habitats are forcing them closer to farms and villages.

CRUSHED TO DEATH?

The elephant then began to use her body to crush him. Adrenaline was coursing through Fay, so he didn't feel any pain even as he heard the sound of one of his ribs breaking. He knew he was moments away from death.

Suddenly the elephant changed tactics. She started to get up, allowing Fay to get some air back into his lungs. He was holding onto her tusks for dear life. As long as he could hold on, she couldn't use them to stab him. He knew if he let go, she would kill him. In her fury the elephant tried to shake him off. She flung her massive head from side to side and up and down.

Fay held on. He later recalled he felt like a rodeo rider on a bucking bronco. The elephant shook him around like a rag doll. His girlfriend watched in horror and saw his body going up and down, over and over.

A LUCKY ESCAPE

Fay lost his grip. He went flying and traveled at least 10 feet (3 m) before slamming into the ground. He landed on all fours, shaking and exhausted. At any moment he expected to feel the elephant's tusks plunging into his back. He could hear the sound of his friends shouting at the elephant as he turned around and prepared to face her again.

But she was gone. His friends succeeded in scaring her off—the ordeal was over! Fay saw the blood on the ground and realized for the first time he was injured. There was a long, deep gash in his left arm, nearly down to the bone. His other arm had been punctured all the way through, and there were gashes on both legs—but he had survived!

Michael Fay

WETLAND HORROR
DIANA TILDEN-DAVIS

What's the most dangerous animal in Africa? If you ask around, many people would probably guess a lion. Others might suggest a leopard or crocodile or even a gorilla or venomous snake. Very few people would guess the correct answer—the hippopotamus. These lumbering giants may seem comical, but they are vicious killers. Every year they are responsible for hundreds of fatal attacks on humans in Africa—more than any other animal.

INTO THE WILD

To many people, Diana Tilden-Davis probably seemed like an unlikely person to take on an angry hippo. She was a former beauty pageant contestant who was crowned Miss South Africa in 1991. Later in that same year, she finished as a runner-up in the Miss World pageant.

But for Tilden-Davis, life was more than just swimsuits and hair spray. She grew up in southern Africa and had a deep love for its natural beauty and wildlife. After a brief career as an actress, Tilden-Davis swapped glamour for the outdoors. She started a new life as a tour guide in the Okavango Delta. After years working there, it felt like home to her.

BEAUTIFUL DELTA

The Okavango Delta in Botswana is one of the world's natural treasures. Instead of flowing into the sea, the Okavango River spreads out into a wide delta. Each year it floods the land and turns it into a wetland. Channels of shallow water flow through tall reeds and grasses. The delta is the perfect home to animals, such as elephants, crocodiles, cranes, zebras, and many more. They come there each year to drink and feed. Hippos like to wallow and graze in the shallow waters.

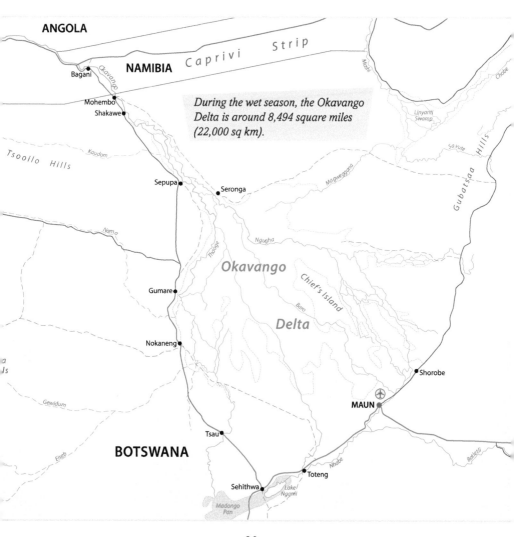

During the wet season, the Okavango Delta is around 8,494 square miles (22,000 sq km).

DANGEROUS WATERS

Just a week or so before Tilden-Davis's encounter, there was another attack in the area. On December 9, 2003, Janice Bartlett and Bruce Simpson were traveling through the delta. The couple from Cape Town, South Africa, was on their honeymoon. A local guide took them through the delta in a small canoe called a mokoro. The guide stood in the back and pushed the mokoro with a pole.

The group came across a herd of elephants blocking their path. This was just the type of wildlife they had come to see! They waited, but the elephants refused to budge. So the guide turned the mokoro around. He took a different path, down another channel hemmed in by reeds.

Out of nowhere, something big exploded out of the water toward them. A large hippo charged their boat and tipped them into the water. The hippo gave Bartlett a vicious bite that went through her heart and lung. She died almost instantly.

CROWDED CONDITIONS

A drought that year meant that the Okavango Delta was drier than normal. These conditions forced animals into smaller areas to look for food. There was less food available overall, and the hippos were stressed. Hungry and forced to cluster closer together than normal, they became irritated and aggressive. Fights were common, especially among the males.

On December 17, Tilden-Davis was on the water in the same area that Bartlett had been attacked. She was poling a mokoro, accompanied by a camera crew. They were filming a documentary and wanted to get one more shot before finishing for the day. But lurking in the shallow waters, where they couldn't see it, was a hippopotamus.

Hippos open their mouth to appear aggressive and intimidating.

ATTACK!

Without warning, the hippo broke the surface and charged the boat. Tilden-Davis knew exactly how dangerous an angry hippo could be. With the long pole used to push the boat along, she attacked the hippo, while shouting at her companions to get to safety.

Hippos normally hang out in herds, often led by one male who is in charge. Younger males may try to take over, leading to vicious fights. If they're not successful, they may be driven out. This could be what happened to the hippo that attacked Tilden-Davis. As it went for her, with its huge mouth open, she could see cuts and gashes in its mouth. There were also wounds on its face, and its ear was chewed. Tilden-Davis could tell these marks were recent—the hippo had been in a serious fight.

FIGHTING FOR SURVIVAL

As the rest of the group scrambled away, the hippo rammed the mokoro. Tilden-Davis fell onto her back in the boat. Then the hippo attacked again. This enormous beast weighed at least 2 tons. Its deadly jaws snapped together inches away from her. Desperate to survive, Tilden-Davis continued to fight back.

IN THE JAWS OF THE BEAST

The hippo bit deep into Tilden-Davis's leg, just above the ankle. She knew she was in danger of being dragged underwater. Even though the waters were fairly shallow, she could easily drown if the hippo didn't let go.

As her crew looked on in horror, Tilden-Davis continued to fight the angry hippo, eventually freeing her leg. The crew's shouts may have scared it away. When the hippo moved on, Tilden-Davis was left bleeding in the bottom of the mokoro.

a hippo in the Okavango Delta

DID YOU KNOW?

Despite their aggressive personality, hippos aren't fierce predators. They graze on grasses and other plants and only eat meat if no other food is available. A hippo has flat molars for grinding plants. Its fearsome tusks, on the other hand, are used for fighting, not for feeding. The tusks can reach over 1 foot (0.3 m) in length and are sharpened every time the hippo closes its mouth. Combined with the animal's huge mouth and powerful bite, these tusks can be deadly.

RUSHED TO THE HOSPITAL

The hippo had bitten through bone and flesh and nearly severed his victim's leg. Members of her crew gave Tilden-Davis first aid while they waited for a helicopter to arrive. As she was loaded onto the airlift, she asked them not to go after the hippo. She said the attack was no one's fault.

At the hospital, doctors raced to repair the damage to Tilden-Davis's leg. They were able to set her broken bone and gave her antibiotics to fight any infection caused by the bite. Over the following weeks and months, she needed further operations to repair the damage caused by the hippo's tusks.

RECOVERY AND FORGIVENESS

Nearly two years later, Tilden-Davis still walked on crutches. She had a metal pin in her leg and more surgeries planned. She was unable to return to her job as a wildlife guide. But she doesn't hold a grudge against the hippo that changed her life. She has actually seen it twice since the ordeal. She knew a hippo wouldn't normally attack like that unless it was in a desperate situation. In the difficult drought conditions that year, she said it probably went through just as hard a time as she did.

Tilden-Davis competing at the Miss World pageant in 1991

DEADLY SWARM
VERN ROBERTS

Hippos, elephants, bears, and great white sharks are very large animals. But not all deadly animals are big. In fact, some of them are very small! Scorpions and snakes can kill, and bees sting to defend their hives. A single sting is painful, and unless the victim is allergic, it's not life-threatening. However, bees occasionally attack in large swarms, and these attacks can turn deadly, as Vern Roberts discovered.

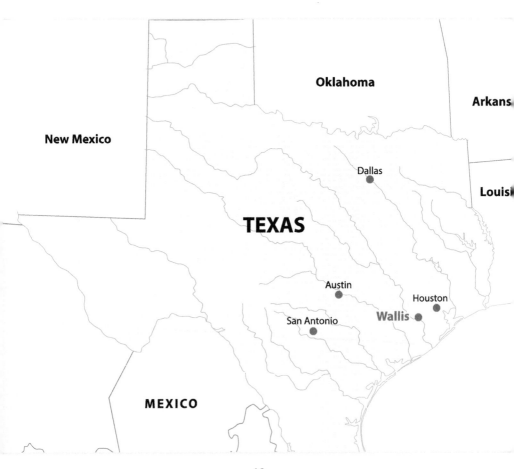

JUST A NORMAL DAY

Roberts lived in the small town of Wallis in southeastern Texas. It was a typical day in September, and he was mowing his lawn. He made his way around the yard when he felt something small hit his head. That impact was followed by another, and then another.

Roberts quickly realized bees were stinging him. They came out of the grass, probably reacting to the noise and vibrations of the lawnmower. He swatted at them and quickly decided it would be better to get away. But the bees wouldn't leave him alone.

KILLER BEES

Roberts was attached by Africanized honeybees—often known as "killer bees." They are a cross between the African and European species of honeybee. These hybrid bees are not very big. In fact they're smaller than the European honeybees found throughout North America. Their stings carry less venom.

Unlike their gentler cousins, Africanized bees are very aggressive. They attack in large swarms when their hive is under threat. A honeybee can only sting a person once, because its stinger is usually torn off in the process. It would take about 1,000 bees to deliver enough toxin to kill a grown adult with no bee allergies. Unfortunately for Roberts, "killer bees" are known to attack in these kinds of numbers.

FAIR-WEATHER FOES

Africanized honeybees first appeared in South America and slowly spread north. By the 1990s, they reached the southern part of the United States, where temperatures are warm. Africanized honeybees can't cope with cold weather like European honeybees can. Southern Texas, where Roberts lived, was killer bee country, and there was a history of attacks.

SWARM!

Roberts shouted and tried to get away from the bees that swarmed around him. They stung him all over his body: on his arms, in his ears and even in his mouth and throat. Each sting was a separate stab of agonizing pain. Roberts tried everything he could think of to get rid of the bees, including the "stop, drop, and roll" technique. Nothing seemed to work, and he began to feel overwhelmed by the attack.

Africanized honeybees are also called killer bees.

Roberts' wife, Mary, was inside the house. When she heard his screams, she rushed outside. To her horror, she saw her husband covered in bees.

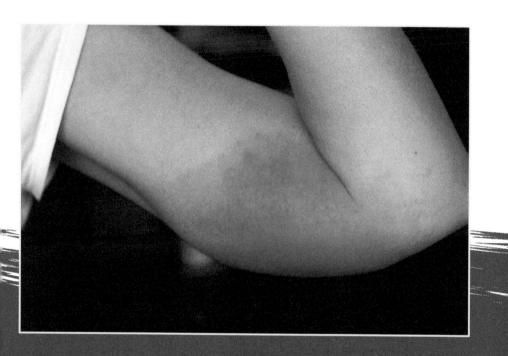

DID YOU KNOW?

When a bee stings you, it injects venom into your body. The venom dissolves and spreads quickly. It can destroy cells, including blood cells. A chemical in the venom triggers your body to release a substance called histamine. Histamines are part of the body's natural defense system. They help rid the body of dangerous substances. After a bee sting, histamine makes the surrounding area swollen and tender.

OVERWHELMED

Roberts was on the ground, covered in stinging bees. Mary tried to get to him, but the bees stung her as well. Every time Roberts managed to stand and start for the house, the furious swarm of bees brought him down to the ground again. He could hardly see past the pain and fear, but he was determined to hang on for Mary's sake.

With Mary's help, Roberts was able to stagger into the house. They called 911, but when the ambulance arrived, the paramedics couldn't get to them. The bees were still swarming around, and it wasn't safe for them to leave the ambulance. Roberts and Mary knew if they wanted help, there was only one thing to do. They walked out of the house and through the bees to get to the ambulance, suffering even more stings as they went.

INTENSIVE CARE

At the hospital doctors treated the couple for their injuries. Mary was stung more than 40 times and was in a lot of pain. But that was nothing compared to her husband. Vern had more than 600 stings covering his body. His arms and legs were swollen, and he was in extreme pain. When the doctors took off his jeans, his legs looked like they were covered in confetti—but the specks were actually bee stingers.

The doctors removed the stingers, and Roberts spent three days in the intensive care unit. The stings gradually healed, and the swelling went down. Roberts eventually made a full recovery. But he was determined to make one change in his life: from now on, when he mows the lawn, he will wear a protective beekeeper's suit!

Some emergency responders, including firefighters, wear protective clothing to keep them safe from bee stings.

KILLER CAT

ANNE HJELLE

The animal with the scientific name *Puma concolor* goes by many names: puma, cougar, panther, catamount, mountain lion. But no matter what you call them, these wild cats are deadly. They are not as big as lions or tigers, but they can take down prey larger than themselves. Thirty-year-old mountain biker Anne Hjelle discovered that one day in 2004, when she barely escaped a vicious attack.

ON THE TRAIL

Hjelle was a former Marine who worked as a personal trainer. A few years before, she had taken up mountain biking. The hobby was a perfect match for her personality. She loved the chance to spend time outdoors and push her body to the limit.

On January 8, 2004, she was in the Whiting Ranch Wilderness Park in southern California, not far from where she lived. This 2,500-acre (1,012-hectare) park is popular with hikers and mountain bikers, and Hjelle often rode there. She loved the forested trails and steep slopes. On the day of the attack, she was riding with a friend, Debi Nicholls.

READY TO RIDE

During a hard climb up a steep road, Hjelle and Nicholls chatted. Once at the top, Hjelle saw two other bikers start down the Cactus Hill trail. That roused her competitive nature—she considered that trail to be part of her own territory. With Nicholls right behind her, she started down the trail. If she could ride hard and fast, she might catch up with the other riders.

Hjelle came around a blind corner and found a man stopped on the trail. He was on one bike and held another. Hjelle stopped to ask him if everything was all right. He said he had found an abandoned mountain bike on the trail.

JUST A JOKE?

Hjelle figured the man was joking. She thought he was one of the two riders she had seen at the top, and that his partner was taking a bathroom break in the woods. Nobody knew that earlier in the day another biker had been killed by a mountain lion on that very trail. The abandoned bike was his, and the mountain lion was still out there.

Blissfully unaware, Hjelle continued down the trail. It wasn't long before she spotted a flash of movement over her right shoulder. She saw reddish-brown fur and assumed she had startled a deer. But just a few seconds later, something rammed into her with the force of a truck. Hjelle was carried off her bike and slammed into the ground. That's when she realized something incredibly strong grabbed her by the head.

FIGHTING FOR HER LIFE

Hjelle knew this type of attack could only come from a mountain lion. These predators were sometimes spotted in the park, though they hardly ever went after humans. The cat bit the back of her neck and was trying to drag her off the path and into the forest.

Nicholls caught up and was shocked at what she saw. She screamed for help, jumped off her bike, and threw it at the mountain lion. But the bike got caught up in the bushes and didn't hit the target. Nicholls then threw herself down on the ground and grabbed Hjelle by her left leg. She hung on for dear life.

a mountain lion

DID YOU KNOW?

Mountain lions are the biggest cats in the United States. They often hunt large animals such as deer and elk. These large cats use stealth to sneak up on their prey and use their powerful back legs to pounce. They have a very powerful bite, and they can sever the spinal cord or break the neck of their prey with a single bite.

DRAGGED

Despite Nicholls' efforts, the big cat dragged both women into the woods, toward a ravine. It would drag Hjelle for a few feet, then stop and adjust its grip. Its first bite had been on the back of her neck. The next was on the side of her head, and Hjelle could feel her ear come away from her skull.

The vicious attack was far from over. The next time the mountain lion bit her, its teeth tore into the left side of her face. Hjelle could feel her cheek tear away—a large flap of skin was now hanging loose. She later recalled the animal's sharp teeth tore into her flesh as easily as a hot knife through butter. She knew how much damage the cat had done to her face, and for a split second felt she didn't want to live. But then her thoughts turned to her husband. He would want her to fight.

JAWS OF DEATH

Unfortunately there wasn't much she could do against such a strong attacker. With one arm she reached over her shoulder to punch the mountain lion in the head. It had no effect. Then the lion let go of her face and bit down on the front of her neck. Hjelle couldn't breathe, and she felt herself starting to black out. "I'm going to die," she told Nicholls. But her friend shouted back that she would never let her go.

The next thing Hjelle knew, she was on her back in the woods, struggling to breathe. Alerted by the screams, other mountain bikers came to help. They threw rocks at the mountain lion until one hit it in the head. The mountain lion released Hjelle and ran off. Although the lion was gone, she couldn't get any air into her lungs. She was choking on her own blood.

Mountain lions often attack and kill prey by biting its neck.

RESCUE

Nicholls helped Hjelle sit up to clear her airways. She worked to get her breathing under control. Another biker helped Nicholls carry Hjelle back up to the path, and someone called 911. When the paramedics came, they brought her out to where a helicopter could collect her.

As the helicopter took off, the pilot spotted what he thought was a body in the woods. He radioed the police, who sent a team to investigate. The searchers found the body of 35-year-old Mark Reynolds, who had been killed and partially eaten by the mountain lion before it attacked Hjelle. Later that day two sheriff's deputies shot and killed the 110-pound (50 kg) mountain lion responsible for the attacks.

Anne Hjelle

LASTING SCARS

In the hospital, it took doctors several hours and about 200 stitches to even begin to repair the damage to Hjelle's face, neck, and chest. They counted as many as 40 different bite wounds, some of them several inches deep. One of the bites went all the way from the front of her throat to the back of her neck, touching the vertebrae.

Over the years that followed, Hjelle had a series of reconstructive operations, but the scars of the attack remain. Aside from adjusting to her changed appearance, one of the hardest things for Hjelle was going back to the woods where the attack happened. She made several trips back to the attack site: first on foot, with armed police, and then on a bike with her husband and other riders. Finally she was able to face the trail with just one other friend.

Several years after the attack, Hjelle and her husband had their first child. It was a girl, whom they named Elsa. But she's not named after the Disney princess—she's named after a different film character. The 1966 film *Born Free* tells the true story of a couple who raise an orphaned lion cub and release it into the wild. The lion's name? Elsa!

GLOSSARY

adrenaline—a substance that is released in the body causing the heart to beat faster and giving more energy

delta—the triangle-shaped area where a river deposits mud, sand, and pebbles

drought—a long period of weather with little or no rainfall

ingenuity—skill, creativity, and resourcefulness

intensive care unit—a department in a hospital where patients who need constant care and observation are treated

IV—a medical apparatus consisting of tubes and a needle that allows fluids to be injected directly into a patient's bloodstream; short for intravenous

oxygen—a colorless gas in the air that people and animals need to breathe

poacher—a person who hunts or fishes illegally

regulator—a piece of equipment that allows divers to breathe air from an air tank

tourniquet—a tight wrapping designed to prevent a major loss of blood from a wound

transfusion—the act of transferring blood or other fluids into the veins of a person who needs it

vertebrae—the small bones that surround and protect the spinal cord

wildfire—a large, destructive fire that spreads quickly over woodland or brush

READ MORE

Marsico, Katie. *Surviving a Shark Attack: Bethany Hamilton.* Minneapolis, MN: Lerner Publications, 2019.

Mason, Paul. *The Shark Attack Files.* Minneapolis, MN: Hungry Tomato, 2018.

Ventura, Marne. *How to Survive an Animal Attack.* Mankato, MN: Child's World, 2015.

INTERNET SITES

Animal Attack Statistics
edition.cnn.com/2016/06/17/health/animal-attacks-statistics/index.html

The 10 Most Dangerous Animals in the World
www.cntraveler.com/stories/2016-06-21/the-10-most-dangerous-animals-in-the-world

What to Do When a Wild Animal Attacks
www.nytimes.com/2016/06/27/travel/animal-attack-mountain-lion-alligator.html

SOURCE NOTES

p. 8, "I got attacked..." Bethany Hamilton, in an interview with Oprah Winfrey, 2004, https://www.youtube.com/watch?v=ffgxXjGPrT4, 00:44. Accessed January 22, 2019.

p. 10, "Oh please . . . not..." Dad of Teen Who Lost Arm Was Set for Knee Surgery, *Deseret News*, November 5, 2003, https://www.deseretnews.com/article/525035807/Dad-of-teen-who-lost-arm-was-set-for-knee-surgery.html. Accessed on January 22, 2019.

p. 57, "I'm going to die..." Anne Hjelle, in an interview on the Joy in My House radio program, https://www.youtube.com/watch?v=dK1V-GDpWwM, 33:40. Accessed on January 28, 2019.

BIBLIOGRAPHY

"Extreme Hippo Attack: Extreme Hippo Attack - Biggest Human Threat in Africa," Endangered Animals, June 22, 2015, https://www.youtube.com/watch?v=KzZ9aRkIxBE Accessed on April 18, 2019.

"I Survived A Mountain Lion Attack," SoulPancake, June 21, 2018, https://www.youtube.com/watch?v=h8_W928jGO8 Accessed on April, 18, 2019.

"Long Road to Recovery for Former Beauty Queen," IOL, January, 2, 2004, https://www.iol.co.za/news/south-africa/long-road-to-recovery-for-former-beauty-queen-119723 Accessed on April 18, 2019.

"Species Implication in Shark Attacks," Florida Museum, August 2, 2018, https://www.floridamuseum.ufl.edu/shark-attacks/factors/species-implicated/ Accessed on April 18, 2019.

"Swarm of More Than 300 African Bees Attack Couple in Wallis," ABC 13 News, September 18, 2018, https://abc13.com/swarm-of-more-than-300-bees-attack-couple-in-wallis-/4279174/ Accessed on April 18, 2019.

Biography.com Editors, "Bethany Hamilton Biography" Biography.com, June 5, 2015, https://www.biography.com/people/bethany-hamilton Accessed on April, 18, 2019.

Burton, Connie, "Arizona Bear Attacks Up to Three in a Month," ABC News, June 26, 2012, https://abcnews.go.com/blogs/headlines/2012/06/arizona-bear-attacks-up-to-three-in-a-month/ Accessed on April 18, 2019.

Brown, Patricia Leigh, "Surfer on Her Way Up, Brought Down by a Shark," *The New York Times*, November 4, 2003, https://www.nytimes.com/2003/11/04/us/surfer-on-her-way-up-brought-down-by-a-shark.html Accessed on April 18, 2019.

Chadwick, Alex, "An Explorer's Harrowing Encounter," NPR, January 8, 2003, https://www.npr.org/templates/story/story.php?storyId=907352 Accessed on April 18, 2019.

Fay, Michael, "What It Feels Like...to Be Attacked by an Elephant," *Esquire Magazine*, July 16, 2007, https://www.esquire.com/lifestyle/a3162/elephant0807/ Accessed on April, 18, 2019.

Lake, Kari, "Exclusive: Arizona Man Survives Savage Bear Attack, Shares Story of Survival," Fox 10 News, May 4, 2016, http://www.fox10phoenix.com/news/arizona-news/bear-attack Accessed on April 18, 2019.

Mazziotta, Julie, "Couple Stung Around 600 Times by Bees While Working in Their Yard: 'They Overwhelmed Me'," People, September, 18, 2018, https://people.com/health/bee-attacked-couple-stung-600-times/ Accessed on April 18, 2019.

Stephenson, Alison, "Abalone Diving - The Reward Is High, But the Risk Is Great," News.com.au, June 26, 2013, https://www.news.com.au/entertainment/awards/abalone-diving-the-reward-is-high-but-the-risk-is-great/news-story/748928d723be6a6f005916bfd6792b20 Accessed on April 18, 2019.

Squires, Nick, "Man Whose Head Was 'Swallowed' by Great White Shark Lives to Tell the Tale," *The Telegraph*, January 24, 2007, https://www.telegraph.co.uk/news/worldnews/1540442/Man-whose-head-was-swallowed-by-great-white-shark-lives-to-tell-the-tale.html Accessed on April 18, 2019.

Whiting, David, "Anne Hjelle, Mauled by Mountain Lion 13 Years Ago, Shakes Off Nightmares and Shares Joy of Being a Mom," Orange County Register, June 21, 2017, https://www.ocregister.com/2017/05/12/anne-hjelle-mauled-by-mountain-lion-13-years-ago-shakes-off-nightmares-and-shares-joy-of-being-a-mom/ Accessed on April 18, 2019.

INDEX

ABOUT THE AUTHOR

Nancy Dickmann has written more than 150 nonfiction books for children, specializing in science and history. Before becoming an author, she worked for many years as an editor and publisher of children's books.